UNDERSTAND
HOW TO DRAW DS11

Explore the Life of Ponds, Streams, and Rivers

Benjamin Perkins

SEARCH PRESS

Introduction

Water, with its glancing lights, ripples, and reflections, enhances any scene. It also attracts a tremendous diversity of life-forms, from mammals and birds, reptiles and amphibians, and handsome insects such as dragon-flies and damselflies, to the fish and insect larvae which inhabit its depths and the myriad tiny organisms which make up the plankton. The waterside vegetation is no less varied and interesting, with lovely flowers such as water-lilies and marsh marigolds, beds of plumed reeds and bulrushes, and trees which lean out over the water, their foliage filtering the light and casting dappled shadows across pond or stream. If the water is still, then it may mirror them faithfully, but if flowing or wind-ruffled then the reflections will be contorted and fragmented. For the artist, the waterside provides infinite opportunities and challenges, and the options are many, from a broad landscape treatment to detailed depictions of plant and animal life.

In this book, I describe how I tackle the different aspects of drawing pond, stream, and river life, but I think that it is important to point out that every individual will, in time, develop a style and technique that is to some extent unique. No two artists interpret any scene in exactly the same way – that is what makes painting and drawing such fun – and although we are all influenced by the work of others, particularly masters of the craft, slavish imitation should be avoided. Draw in the style that suits you best and expresses your own individuality.

The most important piece of advice that I can give is that you should get into the habit of drawing as much as possible directly from nature. Always have a small sketch-book and pencil with you, and draw at every opportunity. There is a spontaneity and dynamism about such sketches that can never be achieved if you work from, for instance, photographs, and

Fox in pen and ink on Bristol board. The fox is heavily shaded in order to make him stand out against the background of the grassy bank. Note that the shadow he casts is also very strongly indicated to help to plant him firmly on the ground.

this should still be apparent even if the sketches are only used as an element in work done later in the studio. Photography does have its uses, however. A dragon-fly, for example, will never sit still long enough for you to make a detailed drawing of its complicated shape and intricate patterns (although quick sketches can still be very useful in establishing its overall appearance and posture). For the detail, artists of an older generation had to rely upon dead specimens, but a photograph is obviously greatly preferable to the use of the killing bottle and can usually be obtained with a little patience. Since composition is an important element in any drawing, you should make a point of using only photographs that you have taken yourself. Photographs can also be used as a back-up to sketches done in the field, since there is not always time to include all the necessary detail, but they should be looked upon as a secondary source, and wherever possible the basis of a finished drawing should be field sketches.

Equipment and materials

For the field, the basic requirements are very simple, consisting merely of a sketch-pad and a pencil. I use a sketch-pad or sketch-book of white cartridge paper, of a size that will fit into a fishing bag (made of stout, weatherproof canvas with handy pockets on the outside). Better still, most art shops sell collapsible stools which incorporate zipped pockets to contain all your sketching gear. I find a hardback sketch-book measuring 21.5 x 15.2cm (8 x 6in) perfect for sketches of birds, animals, and plants, but you will need something rather larger if landscape is your object. Rather than using wooden pencils, which need continuous sharpening, these days I always carry two 0.5 automatic pencils, one with an HB lead and one with a 2B one. In my experience, softer leads smudge too readily for field use.

Some people like to work almost exclusively outdoors. I prefer to do sketches in the field, and finished drawings at home where I am less at the mercy of wind, rain, insects, and changes in light intensity. There is now a wide range of drawing papers available, and you will have to experiment to find the type that suits your style and medium. The ones that I use most frequently are a smooth or semi-smooth white cartridge paper for pencil sketches, smooth Bristol board for fine pen-and-ink work, and a not (slightly rough) watercolour paper for drawings in wash or pen and wash. I also use not paper quite often for pencil work when I require a grainy finish.

I never use any pencil harder than an H grade, and, as mentioned already, I tend to do most of my primary drawing using automatic pencils. For the later stages of a drawing I have a number of traditional wooden-shafted pencils, ranging in grade from B to 6B (the softest), which I find especially useful for cloudy skies and large areas of dark shadow.

You should, of course, try to use an eraser as little as possible, since too much erasing will quickly damage the surface of the paper, but it is still a very necessary tool. I find soft plastic erasers by far the most effective and an improvement on the old India rubber.

For pen-and-ink work you have the choice between nibbed drawing pens, which have the advantage of being able to produce lines which vary in thickness, and automatic pens, which are easier to use and do not have to be continually dipped in ink but only produce a line of constant width.

A favourite drawing method of mine is to use a fine brush with watercolour paint (generally sepia or some shade of grey). The brush has to be of good quality, and it is worth spending money on a well-made sable, which keeps its springiness and a fine point for a long time. Old brushes, which have become blunt, can be used for the broad washes. This method can be used on its own or in conjunction with pen and ink. Use a fairly heavy paper, at least 180gsm (90lb), to avoid any risk of cockling.

Drawing with pastel or charcoal involves rather specialized skills, but many people like to use a ball-point pen or felt- or fibre-tipped pens for drawing, and indeed anything which makes a line can be used. Try them all, and see which suits you best.

Basic techniques

Pencil

In whichever medium I am working, I always begin by lightly pencilling in the main components of the composition. If the whole picture is to be done using some form of pencil, then it is a matter of building up the main areas of light and shade, adding detail, and strengthening the lines of prominent features in the foreground. Unlike watercolour landscapes, where you start with sky and background, there is no fixed rule about where to start and where to finish, but if you are right-handed then it is a good idea to work from top-left to bottom-right, so that the heel of your hand is not smudging the work that you have done already. To obviate this risk further, I find it useful to have a suitably sized square of tracing-paper under my drawing hand. This also prevents the paper from becoming greasy.

Once the composition is established in outline, shadowed areas can be built up using hatching. This consists of a lot of close, more or less parallel, strokes which can be either straight or curved. More pressure will give darker lines, and a uniform effect can be achieved by making the lines contiguous. Progressively darker areas can be created by cross-hatching and also by the use of softer pencils. Contrasts of light and shade can be very important to the success of a picture, and you should bear this in mind when planning the main features of the composition.

Swimming pike. Pen and ink on cartridge paper.

Pen and ink

Exactly the same techniques apply when using pen and ink, although the contrasts in this medium tend to be more severe and call for greater skill in order to capture the gradations between light and dark. One way of overcoming this is to combine the use of pen and ink with black crayon or Conté. Delicate lines and fine hatching will require a fine-nibbed pen, whilst for very dark areas and stronger hatching, you will need a thicker nib or even, for the totally dark areas (silhouettes), the use of a brush. Of course, intensity of shade can also be varied by making the lines closer or more distant from one another, and by cross-hatching.

Great diving beetle. HB pencil on Bristol board.

Wash

I like to draw using a fine brush and watercolour paint in a colour such as warm sepia, lamp black, or Payne's grey. The point of the brush can be used to draw lines just as effectively as a pen or a pencil, and broader strokes of the brush create the shadowed areas. You can use this technique on its own, having first sketched in the outlines of the composition in pencil, or in conjunction with pen and ink.

Any drawings done in pencil or other soft media, such as charcoal, will need fixing in order to prevent smudging, using an aerosol fixative. Make sure that the container is reasonably warm, or the contents will come out in blobs instead of as a fine spray.

Redstart. Watercolour wash on watercolour not paper.

1.

2.

3.

4.

Water and water plants

There are comparatively few plants which are completely aquatic, and some of these, like duckweed, are so small that collectively they appear as a green film on the water surface. Others, like mare's-tail and arrowhead, have interesting shapes which can be used to effect in composing water scenes, particularly in conjunction with waterfowl – for splendid examples, look at the paintings of Charles Tunnicliffe. On ponds and slow-flowing rivers, water-lilies are the most familiar of aquatic plants, whilst the crowded white flowers of water crowfoot are typical of chalk streams. Different plants favour different types of water, so by looking at the plants themselves it is possible to consider the ways of depicting water in its various moods – mirror-calm, fast-flowing, wind-ruffled, and so on. On the opposite page are four examples, all of which have been worked on watercolour not paper using a 2B pencil. Remember that pencil on this type of paper gives a grainy effect; you would obtain a different, smoother effect, and sharper lines, by using a smooth paper.

Reflections in water

An important point to note when depicting the movements of water is that whilst in still conditions the reflections of objects on land will be a perfect mirror image, as the wind increases and the ripples or wavelets get larger and closer together, so they will reflect more of the sky, and the reflections from the land will become ever more elongated and fragmented until, in choppy water, they disappear altogether.

Therefore, to give a sense of reality to your drawings of water, it is necessary to emphasize both the horizontals of the water surface and the verticals of reflected objects. Overleaf are three examples, all of which have been worked in HB pencil on smooth cartridge paper.

1. The leaves and flowers of yellow water-lilies on the still surface of a pond. These were drawn looking down at them from quite a high bank. The water was unruffled, and at the top of the picture you can see the reflections of bushes on the opposite bank. The plants were in bright sunlight, but the water was dark under the near bank and gradually became lighter towards the middle of the pond.

2. A highland lake, the water surface barely rippled by a very light breeze, with the spiky stems of horsetail growing in the shallows. For the clouds, I wanted a smoother effect than the 2B pencil can produce on this rather rough paper, so I used a black crayon instead.

3. Fast, shallow water over the pebbly bottom of a chalk stream, with beds of water crowfoot and long, ribbon-like reeds straining in the current. Here, the strong diagonal axis of the drawing is designed to give the impression of the water's fast, uninterrupted flow.

4. Fast water again, but this time running over an uneven bed, its flow diverted by numerous rocks. The result is a mass of swirls and eddies, cross-currents and ripples. There is little aquatic plant life in waters of this type, and what there is is submerged.

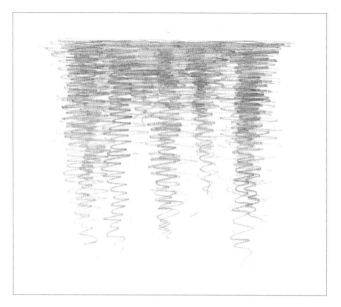

A very simple way to give the impression of reflections in water is to use joined-up horizontal lines, but to produce them in vertical columns corresponding to the objects on the bank.

For reflections in very still water the main emphasis of the lines may be vertical, but there will always be some movement on the water surface (not to mention floating objects) and this can be indicated by light cross-hatching. Here I have also used an eraser to create horizontal streaks representing ripples, such as may be caused by rising fish, hatching insects, and so on.

In rippled water there is often a sheltered area near the bank where the water is calm and the reflections appear strongly. They may peter out quite quickly, however, as the ripples increase when more exposed to the breeze.

Marginal plants

Most ponds and rivers have a rich diversity of plant life at their margins. These consist of reeds, rushes, and sedges, which often grow in dense beds; plants with handsome flowers, such as marsh marigold and yellow flag iris; and bushes and trees, amongst which alders and members of the willow family frequently predominate. When working on a waterside scene the artist should be aware of the individual species, for each has its special characteristics – dark or light foliage, leaf shape, habit of growth, and so on – which can be brought out even in the simplest of sketches to help to give the scene integrity.

Here are three contrasting drawings, in different media, in each of which the bankside vegetation is important, both in setting the context and in creating the desired atmosphere.

This drawing of a lake in winter started out as a very slight pencil sketch on watercolour not paper. It was worked on site and did no more than indicate the main features of the composition: the background fringe of trees, the island reed-beds and lone willow, and the reeds in the foreground. The rest of the work was done at home using a No. 5 sable brush and watercolour paint. The line drawing was done using the point of the brush, and just as you would use the flattened lead of a pencil to provide shading, so the side of the brush was used here for washes and shadowed areas. It is a drawing method of great delicacy, capable of producing fine and flexible lines, and a very wide tonal range. I drew the pale background first, and then worked towards the foreground. Generally speaking, darker lines can be superimposed upon paler ones, but allowance had to be made, in drawing the middle-ground, for the pale plumes of the reeds.

9

In this pencil sketch of a quiet stream running through a lowland, pastoral landscape, the sycamore in the near foreground stands straight, but the young alders on the opposite bank bend slightly in the breeze; flags, growing from the right-hand bank, hang down towards the water, whilst in the background the tall, rather ragged shapes of old white willows rear up against the low skyline. The sketch was done on watercolour not paper using an HB pencil, the darker tones being reinforced with a 2B pencil.

Flowers in detail

When I draw individual flowers in detail, it is usually as a preliminary to painting them – in the case of flowers, I can seldom resist the lure of their colours. This drawing of the flowers of yellow flag iris differs only from such a preliminary drawing in that I have added pencil shading. Always draw flowers from life, so that you can examine their intricate structure as you go along. Drawings done from photographs are too static and, since you cannot observe the flowers from different angles, seldom accurate.

Yellow flag iris. HB and 2B pencils on smooth cartridge paper.

Opposite: a fibre-tipped pen can be used to make pictures rather reminiscent of scraperboard work or woodcuts. Here, the dark trees opposite cast their reflections on the river, creating a backdrop against which the sunlit summer flowers – hogweed, meadowsweet, and willow-herb – stand out. The whole picture was done on smooth cartridge paper using a rather broad-tipped pen, apart from the shading on the flower-heads, which was done with a fine nib.

13

Insects

All ponds and rivers abound with insect life, although the acid waters of upland streams have far fewer species than lowland waters where the vegetation is lush. Many species spend the greater part of their lives as aquatic nymphs and then enjoy a brief period of flight, during which they mate, before they die. Most of these species are comparatively small, the largest being the hawker dragonflies, and when I do drawings of them it is usually for my natural history diary rather than in the cause of picture-making. I make a note of their size, but generally draw them rather larger than life and with the aid of a magnifying glass.

When drawing small, complicated organisms, always start with the outline, taking care that the relative proportions of its component parts are accurately reflected, and then add the shading and details such as the venation of the wings. Here are three examples, all of which have been worked in HB pencil on Bristol board.

1. This is the empty skin of a stone-fly nymph, one of the species that does favour stony upland waters. I found it attached to a rock, and brought it home in a matchbox so that I was able to make an accurate drawing of it under very easy circumstances. The adult insect had emerged through the split in the back.

2. Live insects obviously present more of a problem, but the mayfly, of which this is the 'spinner' or final stage, will sometimes rest for a time on an upright reed or sedge. Even so, it would be very difficult to make a detailed drawing, such as this, in the field, and the only alternative is to capture the insect and imprison it briefly in a glass receptacle.

3. Similarly, with an underwater creature such as this great diving beetle, the best method is to draw it whilst it is temporarily confined in an aquarium – or a jam jar. Here, the beetle is resting on the leaves of watercress.

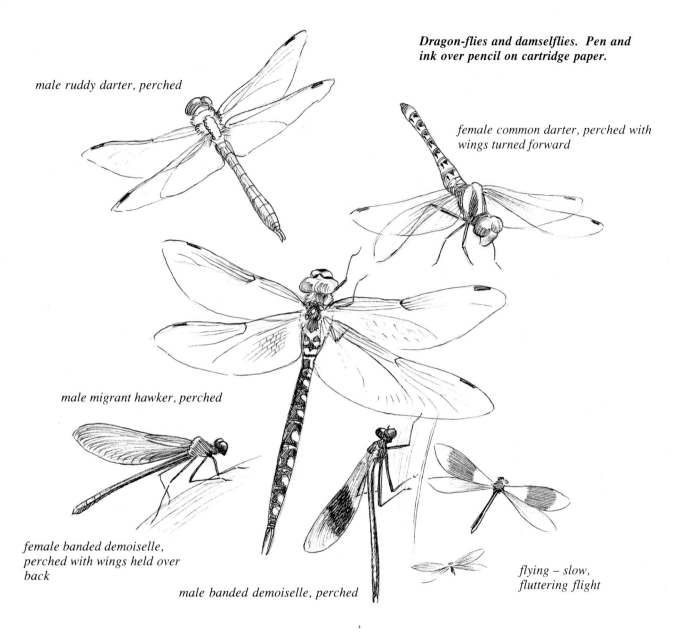

male ruddy darter, perched

Dragon-flies and damselflies. Pen and ink over pencil on cartridge paper.

female common darter, perched with wings turned forward

male migrant hawker, perched

female banded demoiselle, perched with wings held over back

male banded demoiselle, perched

flying – slow, fluttering flight

Of all the insects associated with ponds and rivers, dragon-flies and damselflies are perhaps the most attractive. With their brilliant colours, I always long to paint them, perhaps as an adjunct to a botanical painting, but accurate drawing is an essential first step towards this aim. Dragon-flies are large enough and sufficiently abundant to be sketched quite easily in the field. Such sketches (see above) are useful in showing typical outlines and perching positions, but you cannot hope

15

Southern hawker dragon-fly. Watercolour wash on watercolour not paper.

to capture, in a quick sketch, the details of anatomical structure, wing venation, or colour markings. To produce this detailed drawing, done with a No. 5 sable brush and watercolour paint, of a southern hawker dragon-fly perched on a stem of hogweed, I had to use a photograph which I had taken in my garden.

Butterflies are not specifically water creatures, and no part of their life cycle is aquatic, but they are seldom absent from any waterside scene during the summer months. Like dragon-flies, they are highly decorative insects. Once again, sketches in the field are helpful in capturing the lifelike pose – too often

butterflies in paintings and drawings look stiff and unnatural, like set specimens (which is what they probably were) – but for the detail you will need either a photograph or the dead insect. To draw, rather than paint, a butterfly is certainly a good exercise in depicting tonal values. To illustrate the point, on the opposite page is a drawing of two butterflies, a Peacock and a Large White, feeding on the flower-heads of hemp agrimony, a common waterside plant. It is not possible to reveal their true colours, but by varying the pressure (this drawing was done entirely with an HB pencil) you can give an accurate impression of markings and tones.

Peacock butterfly (left) and Large White butterfly (right).
HB pencil on Bristol board.

Small water creatures

Most of the sketches I do of small water creatures, such as fish and amphibians, are either to illustrate entries in my natural history diaries, or for reference to be used later in watercolour paintings. For both purposes accuracy is needed – a gudgeon must look like a gudgeon, and a frog must demonstrate that it is a frog and not a toad – whilst for the second purpose especially, I try to capture characteristic movements and postures that help to emphasize the creature's individuality.

Fish are not easy to draw when alive and in their natural habitat, generally presenting only a dorsal view and seldom staying to pose when you approach them too closely. The best way is to catch them with a shrimping net (children are more adept than adults at this) and keep them in a glass aquarium on your desk. This was how I drew the gudgeon illustrated on the opposite page, although the stickleback was done from a freshly dead specimen that I found at the edge of a nearby brook.

Frogs, toads, and newts, with their more complex anatomy, present other problems, particularly as they are often reluctant to sit still when humans are in the vicinity. The frog surrounded by spawn was very amenable, presumably because it was concentrating on spawning at the time. I caught the baby frogs and put them in a white plastic container for the brief period that I needed to sketch them, whilst I drew the newts in midsummer when they had left the water and were torpid during the heat of the day. I put one of them into water briefly, in order to get the typical underwater floating position. The toad, however, was determined to keep moving, crawling doggedly through the grass towards its spawning pond and the nearest female toad.

A crawling toad provides a good exercise for sketching moving animals from life, because its movements are slow and deliberate. The art of drawing a moving creature – and it is one which comes only from prolonged practice – is to obtain a mental 'snapshot' of the animal in a characteristic pose, and to translate it on to the paper as quickly as possible, before it fades. This involves using a minimum of clean, accurate lines, outlining the shape of the body, limbs, and any other salient features such as, in the case of a frog or a toad, the bold ridge between shoulder and hip. It is essential – although often difficult – to get the proportions right: the size of the head and length of the limbs in relation to the body; the depth of the body showing below and above the lateral ridge; the distance of the eye-sockets from the end of the snout, and from the back of the cranium; and so on. Once you have established an accurate outline sketch, the battle is nearly won. Details, such as the eye, and the warts and creases on the skin, can be added at leisure (if necessary, in the case of a toad, by detaining it briefly in some suitable receptacle), whilst the shadows and background can be put in last of all.

The more sketches that you do, from different angles and with the animal in various positions, the better. I cannot emphasize enough that continual practice in sketching from life is the essence of all wildlife drawing.

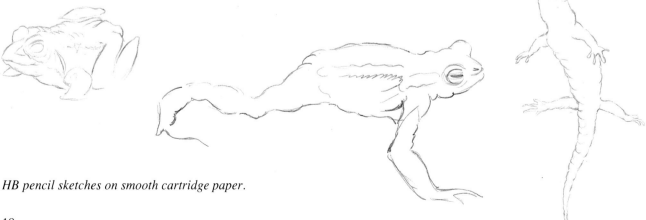

HB pencil sketches on smooth cartridge paper.

Pencil sketches on smooth cartridge paper.

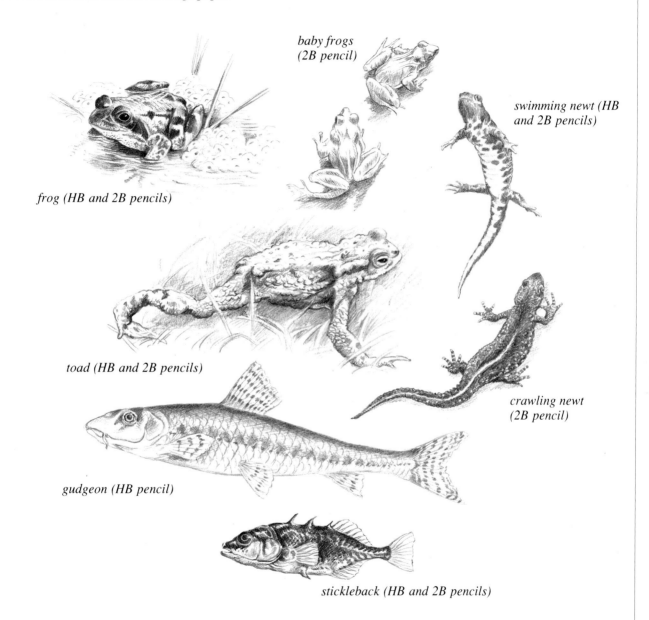

*baby frogs
(2B pencil)*

*swimming newt (HB
and 2B pencils)*

frog (HB and 2B pencils)

toad (HB and 2B pencils)

*crawling newt
(2B pencil)*

gudgeon (HB pencil)

stickleback (HB and 2B pencils)

kingfisher

tufted ducks

white-fronted goose

HB and 2B pencil sketches on smooth cartridge paper.

20

Water birds

Some water birds, such as mute swans, Canada geese, and domestic or semi-domestic ducks and geese, have little fear of humans and, therefore, make excellent subjects for the beginner. Most people know of a park or a river where there are waterfowl, and they can generally get close enough to the birds, not only to be able to make quick outline sketches, but also to fill in the details and tonal variations of the plumage. Bird reserves, where there are hides, provide good opportunities for sketching shy, wild birds, but these generally entail the use of binoculars, and the time-lag between observing the birds and getting your impressions down on paper is necessarily increased, especially if, like me, you need spectacles for drawing. The answer is to spend a long time watching your chosen bird, and impressing all its details and proportions upon your mind, before you begin drawing. Chance encounters in the wild with shy birds, such as kingfishers, call for an even more retentive memory, but however fleeting the glimpse it is still worth making a sketch if you are left with any impression at all of the bird's characteristic outline, whether it was perched, swimming, or flying. Obviously, the more you watch birds, the easier this will become. For example, if you live near a pond where there are moorhens, then, in time, you will become so familiar with their high-stepping gait on land and jerky movements through the water, the white ovals under their cocked tails, and the blobs of sealing-wax red on their bills, that you will be able to make a good attempt at sketching them, even from memory alone.

As with any animal, to be able to draw birds with any conviction it is necessary to have a working knowledge of their anatomy and the way in which their feathers are arranged, so take every opportunity to observe birds of all kinds at close quarters, examine and make sketches from any freshly dead specimens you find, and study the works of great bird artists such as Tunnicliffe, Thorburn, and Bruno Liljefors.

On the opposite page, I have tried to illustrate the use that can be made of quite simple field sketches. The tufted ducks, sitting out on the quiet waters of a mere on a misty day, presented few details, but the shape of their bodies, with tail feathers depressed, rather high-domed heads, and large beaks, together with the bold black and white patterning of the males, make them instantly recognizable. The sketch of the white-fronted goose demonstrates how a quick sketch can contain all of the information necessary for producing a more finished drawing later: the outline of the bird, main features such as the division between wing and flank feathers, and a few lines to indicate the positioning of the most prominent layers of plumage. With this to work from, I had only to add shading to produce what appears to be a much more elaborate drawing. You have to be lucky to get more then a brief glimpse of a kingfisher. If time is short, then try to get down on paper the main elements which go to make up the bird's overall shape. In this case there are just three: the head and beak, the wings from shoulder to tip of primaries, and the tail and under-side from feet to throat. Take great care to reflect accurately the relative proportions of these three elements, and you will have captured at least the basic outline of the bird. Then, if the bird continues to pose, you can start to add details such as the position of the eye, plumage patterns, and so on. The chances are that it will not sit still long enough for you to complete all of the details, but the more that you study birds, the more you will learn and remember about the plumage peculiarities of each species.

After a little practice at drawing birds, you may want to put them into a landscape setting, and here the options, both as to the scene you choose and the style and medium in which you depict it, are vast. On the following pages are three examples.

In this drawing of a group of Canada geese with young, swimming in a brick-walled moat, the adult birds are rather anxious, two of them swimming quite fast with their necks inclined forwards. The drawing was done on Bristol board using pen and ink. In order to indicate its darker tone, I also shaded over the water surface with a grey crayon (incidentally, helping the birds to stand out against their background).

This drawing, in brush and watercolour wash on watercolour not paper, is of a marshland lake, with two avocets, handsome in their black and white plumage, providing the focal point in the foreground. Further out, a great crested grebe swims away, and groups of ducks sit on the water, whilst in the sky a marsh harrier flies up out of the reeds, one foot grasping a water vole. Here, my object was to evoke the atmosphere of a low-flying, bird-haunted marshland scene, and its special interest for me lay in seeking to reproduce the ripples and reflections caused by the avocets wading through the foreground shallows. In the bright water, the reflections of the birds' shadowed under-sides were dark, not white.

This drawing of three swans started out as a pencil sketch on Bristol board – the two females are floating serenely, whilst the cob in the foreground adopts a protective attitude, with its wing feathers arched over its back. The water was very dark, reflecting the trees beyond the reeds, so I used a thick fibre-tipped pen to achieve the deep tone against which the sunlit swans stand out in brilliant whiteness. Finally, I used a fine pen and ink for the details and more muted shadows on the swans themselves, and to tone down their rather dim reflections in the water.

Larger creatures

Of the larger animals – other than birds – which are associated with ponds and rivers, there are only a few – notably the otter, water-vole, and water-shrew – which are truly aquatic, but a majority of mammals swim when necessary and all come to water to drink. Most wild animals are shy, and many nocturnal in their habits, so that in order to observe, let alone sketch, them you will need to be either very lucky or very patient. One way round this problem is to sketch animals in zoos or in special reserves. Domestic animals such as cattle and horses, however, also come to ponds and rivers to drink, and they make excellent subjects for drawing, either on their own or in a landscape context. Make sketches whenever the opportunity occurs – they may well prove useful at some future time when you want to incorporate them into a landscape drawing.

This drawing, in HB and 2B pencils on smooth cartridge paper, started as an outline sketch, which was all I had time for before the horse moved away. Whilst it grazed I could still add details such as the demarcation lines between the brown of the body and the white of blaze and fetlocks, and put in some light shading to indicate muscles and bone structure. The final shading and dappling was done soon after, whilst there was still a strong impression on my mind, although no doubt it would have been less convincing had I not had some previous knowledge of a horse's anatomy and conformation.

This watercolour drawing, on watercolour not paper, depicts bullocks coming down to drink in the shallows of a small river. The cattle liven up the drawing, and at the same time improve the composition. It was a sunny day when I drew this river scene, and this seems a good moment to mention what may appear rather an obvious point – but is sometimes forgotten – that you should always be aware, in any drawing, of the direction of the light source. In this case, the sun shines from the right of the drawing, but fairly high in the sky, as it was around midday when I drew it. As a result, the nearly vertical bank in the foreground is in deep shadow, whilst the more sloping bank beyond it catches the sunlight except where the turf overhangs it, and the trees and bushes on the farther bank are lit up at their forward edges.

Opposite: this 2B pencil drawing of an otter resting but alert originated in a sketch I did at an otter reserve in Suffolk. I then incorporated it in this view of a rocky highland stream where, in fact, otters abound, although they seldom present such a relaxed pose to the onlooker, for they are wary creatures, quickly slipping into the water at the first sight, scent, or sound of an approaching human. The drawing was done on smooth cartridge paper.

I see otters quite frequently whilst fishing in Scotland, but more often than not they are swimming with only their head, and perhaps part of their humped back, exposed, as in this pen-and-ink drawing of an otter forging its way across the rippled water of a pool. The drawing was worked on Bristol board.

To demonstrate how the same sketch can be used in different ways, I have repeated the one of the otter on page 28 in this small drawing of a lowland stream at dusk. Apart from a faint watercolour wash in the sky, it was done with a black ball-point pen on Bristol board. The otter, silhouetted, swims across the lit-up water in the foreground whilst a flock of Canada geese fly overhead. Although the sky, and therefore the water, is still quite light, the trees and reed-beds, together with their reflections, are very dark, giving a sense of evening, the time when otters are most likely to be encountered.

This sketch, in pen and ink on Bristol board, is another example of a watery scene involving an animal. I have placed the water-vole, in characteristic pose nibbling at a piece of reed, in a rather decorative setting. The smooth water, hurrying by towards the right of the picture, is dark, making a good background for the flowers and leaves of the arrowhead and the yellow water-lily.

First published in Great Britain 1993
Search Press Limited,
Wellwood, North Farm Road,
Tunbridge Wells, Kent TN2 3DR

Text and drawings by Benjamin Perkins
Text, illustrations, arrangement, and typography
copyright © 1993 Search Press Limited

Publishers' note
There are references to sable hair brushes in this book. It is the Publishers' custom to recommend synthetic materials as substitutes for animal products wherever possible. There are now a large number of brushes available made of artificial fibres and they are just as satisfactory as those made of natural fibres.

ISBN 0 85532 748 0

Distributors to the art trade:

UK
Winsor & Newton,
Whitefriars Avenue, Wealdstone,
Harrow, Middlesex HA3 5RH

USA
ColArt Americas Inc.,
11 Constitution Avenue,
P.O. Box 1396, Piscataway, NJ 08855-1396

Arthur Schwartz & Co.,
234 Meads Mountain Road, Woodstock, NY 12498

Canada
Anthes Universal Limited,
341 Heart Lake Road South, Brampton, Ontario L6W 3K8

Australia
Max A. Harrell,
P.O. Box 92, Burnley, Victoria 3121

Jasco Pty Limited,
937-941 Victoria Road, West Ryde, N.S.W. 2114

New Zealand
Caldwell Wholesale Limited,
Wellington and Auckland

South Africa
Ashley & Radmore (Pty) Limited,
P.O. Box 2794, Johannesburg 2000

Trade Winds Press (Pty) Limited,
P.O. Box 20194, Durban North 4016

Printed in Spain by A. G. Elkar, S. Coop, 48012 Bilbao